IT'S LONELY AT THE TOP . . .

And no wonder! This gregarious group of corporate despots hand out ulcers along with their annual reports, lose their liberal leanings with their baby fat, and are guarded by secretaries who shoot first and ask questions later!

In PEPPER . . . AND SALT CARTOONS: CEOs AND OTHER KINGS, *The Wall Street Journal*'s zaniest cartoonists turn the corner office upside down to shake loose the craziest collection of CEOs and madcap managers ever to "impact upon" a group of unsuspecting employees. From the boss who communicates only in simple, straightforward buzzwords to the manager who's proving to be as powerful as a golf course sand trap . . . from the corporate dictator who's derailed the company "fast track" to the innovative leader who's substituting Shinto for the Protestant work ethic, you're guaranteed to collect your share of bottom-line delight from the most eccentric executives and maniacal managers ever to have been kicked upstairs.

Pepper...And Salt Cartoons: CEOs And Other Kings

CHARLES PRESTON has been a contributing editor to *The Wall Street Journal* for more than twenty years. He lives in Massachusetts near Cambridge.

THE WALL STREET JOURNAL'S
Pepper...And Salt Cartoons: CEOs And Other Kings

Edited by CHARLES PRESTON

A PLUME BOOK

NEW AMERICAN LIBRARY

NEW YORK AND SCARBOROUGH, ONTARIO

PLUME TRADEMARK REG. U.S. PAT. OFF. AND FOREIGN COUNTRIES
REGISTERED TRADEMARK—MARCA REGISTRADA
HECHO EN SECAUCUS, NEW JERSEY

SIGNET, SIGNET CLASSIC, MENTOR, ONYX, PLUME, MERIDIAN and NAL BOOKS
are published *in the United States* by New American Library,
1633 Broadway, New York, New York 10019,
in Canada by The New American Library of Canada Limited,
81 Mack Avenue, Scarborough, Ontario M1L 1M8

Library of Congress Cataloging-in-Publication Data

The Wall Street Journal's Pepper—and salt cartoons.

    1. Finance—Caricatures and cartoons. 2. American
wit and humor, Pictorial. I. Preston, Charles,
1921–   . II. Wall Street Journal.
NC1428.W33 1986   741.5′973   86-18273
ISBN 0-452-25863-4

First Printing, September, 1986

1 2 3 4 5 6 7 8 9

PRINTED IN THE UNITED STATES OF AMERICA

Where Now, Dow-Jones?

Captains of U.S. industry are riding high.

Not since the Robber Baron days have the perks been so good. However, with the Dow piercing the stratosphere and the bulls leading the pack, the naysayers keep trying to spoil the party. "Remember 1929," they whisper. "This balloon has got to burst. . . ."

No way. Times *have* changed. Even with a stock market "adjustment," the skies will not darken with bodies of brokers and stock analysts careening off skyscrapers.

For this is the era of the Golden Parachute. Any CEO who has maneuvered himself to the top has also designed ingenious routes for his fancy-free fall. In fact, rare is the CEO who accepts the Number One spot without writing in a lucrative escape hatch.

As a chronicle of the bullish eighties, the *Wall Street Journal*'s cartoons offer a witty perspective to life at the top. And there's no arguing that a sense of humor guarantees the highest dividend in the world of business!

—C.P.

"I'd like to give you a raise, but you know what they say about a fool and his money."

1

2   *"Surely you're not going to sign this tissue of lies 'Sincerely yours'!"*

"No, no, Mr. Durbin. This is a business lunch. I'm supposed
to be softening you up, remember?"

3

4

"*Read me the story about Jill and her associate going up the hill.*"

"Don't be alarmed. It's just your ego deflating."

5

6

"He had a very trying day. He invented the wheel, the ambulance, and the legal profession."

"You will meet a tall, dark, handsome man and you will beat him out for a promotion at the office."

7

8

"I envy you, sir. One day, you'll inherit the earth."

"Everyone knows you're a knight in shining armor, but does anyone know who it is that shines your armor?"

9

10

"Do you have any particular predjudice against the smug?"

11

"I'm suing my way through law school."

13

"And as you go out in the world, please remember one thing
. . . pay back your government loans."

14

"And this is my counting room."

16

"You want a divorce? Who's calling?"

"I'm trying to learn to delegate stress."

17

18

"Now then, does anybody else have a stupid suggestion?"

"He's in a very good mood right now, but he won't be if you wake him up."

19

20

"He had a visit from the parent company today."

"*For what Harkness Industries is about to pick up the tab for, may the Lord make us truly thankful.*"

21

"You want recognition? OK—hi!"

"Crampton, would you rewrite this memo using simple, straightforward buzzwords?"

23

24   *"Of course she can handle them. She used to run a day-care center."*

"About my Christmas cards, Miss Rafferty. Please cross out my engraved name and personally sign my name to the one to my mother."

25

26

"If it makes you feel any better, it's lonely at the bottom too!"

"Brooks, this memo shows unusual insight into the human condition."

27

28

"I want you to stop and smell the flowers, Ms. Smith, then write me a report."

29

"When I fired Newsom I had hoped I'd never lay eyes on him again!"

"It's lonely at the top, Harris. But not so lonely that I want
you walking into my office 20 times a day!"

31

"I'll let you know Monday. No point in ruining your weekend."

32

"Of course I don't think of business all the time. I love you. I adore you. I worship the ground you stand on. Read that back to me."

33

"I beat my boss by eight strokes and he says I'm now free to go on the pro tour!"

34

35

36

"*Tell me, Philips. Just how do you fit into the scheme of things?*"

37

38

"Galloway, stop hiding behind that recording and come out in the open!"

"Do you want the grammatical errors in or out?"

39

40

"*Mr. Rafferty has been kicked upstairs. You'll find him on the roof.*"

"As Director of Personnel, I feel I should purchase the robots!"

41

42

"While everyone has been concerned with the quality of life,
I've been busy accumulating the quantity of life."

"Excuse me, sir, but are you maintaining a high profile or a low profile today?"

43

44

"It has been called to my attention, Pettibone, that more and
more of your recent memos have whimsical notes in them."

45

46

"I'm taking you off gut-level decisions. You've got ulcers."

"... And another thing, I'm getting damned sick and tired of always having to take The Hindmost!"

47

48

"Don't tell me he hasn't any talent. Teach him some talent!"

"I have always been a man able to admit his mistakes, and you, Crandal, were a mistake."

49

50

"Look out—he's really on the warpath today!"

51

"*Absolutely no interruptions for the next 20 minutes!*"

52

"Do we accept lottery winners?"

54   *"What I find hard to accept is that there are two sides to every issue."*

"See here, Tom, since when have I become a 'usually reliable source' instead of a 'highly placed source'?"

55

56

BERNHARDT

"You should delegate a little responsibility, Mr. Applewaite."

57

58   *"For $100 you can buy 15 seconds to sell me life insurance."*

"Good presentation, Hotchkiss."

59

"Your medical report says you're healthy as a horse, Windapple. Would you mind explaining how the Vice President in charge of Marketing can do a good job and still be healthy as a horse?"

60

"*Great news, sir! You won the office baseball pool.*"

61

62   *"Come on into my office, Twitters, and let's get right down to mumbo jumbo."*

"I'm sorry, but Mr. Fritch left strict orders not to be disturbed."

63

64   *"The Protestant work ethic isn't cutting it, so we're switching to Shinto."*

"Mr. Wellman, Mr. Archer is holding on line 3 with the Cochran account figures, Ms. Delphin is holding on line 2 with the results of the Hobart survey, and Mr. Clausen is holding on line 5 with a new joke."

65

*"I wouldn't worry about it, Roger, we all start out as liberals.
You lose it with your baby fat."*

66

"Do you have any other identification, sir?"

67

STEIN

68

"You have acquisition fever."

"So, you want to insure your clout?"

69

70

"You say it doesn't work? Are you calling Inspector 23 a liar?"

"Very good, Michael. We'll see you bright and early, ready to
start, Monday, June 30, 1998."

"Watch it. It may be a hostile takeover."

72

"Johnson never could do anything right. He's run off to South America with our accounts payable."

73

"*There's always a place in our organization for a fine, compassionate human being—but he must have the killer instinct, too.*"

"I wish some conglomerate would gobble up this mess!"

75

"My ultimate goal? Retirement."

76

"I can't stand him. He's one of those cooler heads that always prevails."

77

"We've got a dummy corporation. What we need is a smarty corporation."

"... And to those who will become captains of industry ... please keep this faculty in mind if you should be in need of consultants."

79

"*As I mentioned before, Fassler, you'll never go anywhere until you start using 'impact' as a verb.*"

"I had been working late with the computer. It kept calling me stupid, stupid, stupid. I couldn't stand it. I picked up a blunt instrument . . ."

81

82

"It's a miracle the way he keeps his desk so clean."

83

84   *"I'd like to place an ad in your help-wanted section for a workaholic . . . !"*

85

86

"Sometimes I wish I could have a hard day at the office."

"No, I'm not working very hard, just steady."

87

"Don't feel too bad about not doing well in school today. I didn't do so hot in the office today either!"

88

89

90   *"What do you recommend for an expense account that's being audited?"*

"The first thing you should know about our organization is that the buck doesn't stop ANYwhere here."

91

92

"Business administration, eh? Good. I suppose we can teach you the rest of the work: dusting my desk, emptying the wastebasket, etc."

"What a day—it's like a big city out there!"

93

94

"*Mr. Walker is routing my Valentine to all departments. Isn't that sweet!*"

95

96

"However, I should warn you we do discriminate because of inability, ineptitude, and incapacity."

97

98

"I figure if they do fire me, they'll have to pay me a week extra until I clean my office."

99

100

"Mr. Fenster had his resumé prepared by a resumé service, and I'm his stand-in from the same service."

101

"*But surely you must do something else here, Betelman, besides keeping the papers from blowing off your desk.*"

102

"No need to make copies of this memo, Miss Dewlap, just let some of the office gossips read it."

103

*"No, sir, I am not putting you on hold—I am merely transfer-
ring you to a holding mode."*

104

"Mr. Samuels, I feel it is my duty to warn you that Ferrington is back from vacation and he has a beard."

105

106

"That's a coincidence. I dabble a little in accounting."

"Well, what did Mr. Humboldt think of your presentation?"

107

108

"... And when things go wrong I make an ideal scapegoat."

"You have an honest face!"

110

"*Actually, we're looking for somebody who will be eternally grateful for the job.*"

"I threw my back out in a tax dodge."

"Retirement, is OK, except I hate to goof off on my own time."

113

"Mother! Where's your public persona?"

"It's nothing personal, Schraumberg, I just don't feel comfort-able sharing a laboratory with a Capricorn."

115

"That's the difference between the pros and the cons—the pros don't get caught."

"We will now pause for a dozen commercials."

118   *"Gentlemen, I have disquieting news. Our parent company has disowned us."*

"And do you, Debbie, resign yourself to your fate?"

119

120

"*Do we have to go to the party tonight? Mary Trent's gallbladder will be there, and Tom Pierson's ulcers, and Betty Wallace's fibroids, and . . .*"

"As we all know, your uncle was an easy man to rub the wrong way."

121